Growing together

in baptism, eucharist and ministry

A study guide
by William H. Lazareth

Faith and Order Paper No. 114
World Council of Churches, Geneva

Second printing: March 1983

Lay-out and drawings: Claudius Ceccon

Photos: pages 20, 28, 72, 90 and 98 WCC; pages 23, 36 and 68 The Lutheran; pages 24, 32, 77, 92 and 100 World Mission Interpretation; page 48 Leif Gustavsson; page 54 Taizé; page 57 Lutheran World Federation; page 58 Evangelisches Amt für Gemeindedienst; page 62 Vivante Afrique; page 105 CIRIC; page 106 Martin West

Cover design: Nelly Witte-Brooymans
ISBN No. 2-8254-0734-8
© 1982 World Council of Churches,
150 route de Ferney, 1211 Geneva 20, Switzerland
Printed in Switzerland

Table of contents

Introduction

I. Jesus Christ: the way to unity

Jesus Christ declared: "I am the way, the truth and the life." The apostolic Church believed that Christ was both the truth of God's Word and the life of God's world. Moreover, by sharing in that truth and life, persons were inevitably drawn together in Christ's way. Therefore "the way" became a common name for the early Christians to describe their Christ-centred pilgrimage on earth.

Today many Christians want to walk together in that same way. They wish to be visibly united in Christ and with one another in Christ's Church. They believe that it was for this unity that Christ prayed when he asked the Father that his disciples might be one as the Father and the Son are one. God's people, as empowered by the Holy Spirit, are thereby called to reflect the very Tri-unity of God. This is the ultimate ground for both the unity of the Church and the renewal of human community.

We must now ask ourselves whether we truly believe that Church unity is a divine gift and human responsibility that require both ancient recovery and future discovery. Are we convinced that Christ's Church is essentially one — along with being holy, catholic (universal) and apostolic — as we confess in the creed and experience in our local worship and mission? Everything depends on whether we can really affirm that the unity for which Christ prayed already exists, and that the churches are now being called by Christ to become what they actually are: one.

II. Church unity: the goal we seek

The modern ecumenical movement has been inspired by the conviction that visible unity is God's will for the Church. Consequently, recent assemblies of the World Council of Churches have devoted much time to describing the goal of visible Church unity. New Delhi (1961) stressed its local base ("all in each place") and its universal scope ("in all places and all ages"); Uppsala (1968) then further developed its internal relationships ("conciliar fellowship") and its external fulfilment ("sign of the coming unity of humankind").

At Nairobi (1975) the member churches developed the goal still further by declaring that the initial function of the World Council of Churches is "to call the churches to the goal of visible unity in one faith and in one eucharistic fellowship expressed in worship and in common life in Christ, and to advance towards that unity in order that the world may believe". The unity we seek was further described as "a conciliar fellowship of local churches which are themselves truly united".

In the light of recent ecumenical experience, however, must we not admit that we have been far more effective in describing the goal than in realizing it? Why is this so? Perhaps the major reason relates to the fact that it was necessary for Christ to go on to seal his prayer to the Father with his own death and resurrection. Before unity could be fully realized, Christ's body had to be broken and his blood had to be shed. Only then could the Holy Spirit come to work God's life out of our death, God's pardon out of our sin, and God's unity out of our divisions. This lively promise is still at the heart of the Gospel, the new testament of God's coming Kingdom.

Since God's Kingdom is promised to be at hand, are we not first called to repent? Isn't the betrayal of our baptism at the core of the ecumenical dilemma? Aren't we unwilling to die with Christ and aren't we therefore unable to walk in newness of life? Doesn't our disobedience vitiate our discipleship; isn't our diversity corrupted by our divisions? Aren't those divisions perpetuated by our compromises with power and prestige, institutions and investments? Doesn't Church unity ultimately require a future resurrection of our

2

common identity in Christ, following the death of all our present divided identifications?

We must confess before God that we are not yet united together by a common understanding of the apostolic faith. We do not yet share together in one eucharistic fellowship. We are not yet united together in a common ministry. No, we have not yet together achieved the visible Church unity "that the world may believe".

Nevertheless, the Holy Spirit still graciously continues God's forgiving and life-giving work in the Church and the world. It is God the Spirit who makes all things new throughout humanity, history and all creation. Despite the weakness and failures of Christians, the Spirit continues to equip the whole people of God with an abundance of gifts for their varied ministries. The signs of God's reign often seem most evident among those whom our Lord called "the least of these" — the poor, the weak, the suffering and the persecuted. They are frequently manifest in the faithful and loving witness of small groups of Christians, often in very remote parts of the world, in their struggles of daily life and in opposition to the forces of injustice and oppression.

III. Church unity: the steps we take

We now have the opportunity to move towards the goal of Church unity by celebrating some of those interim steps that are being taken together today on the narrow road of ecumenical discipleship. Impressive testimonies abound everywhere. It is the calling of the World Council of Churches to enable and to encourage such ecumenical obedience.

At the same time, we are also compelled to take a hard look at some of the obstacles — sectarian detours and even idolatrous roadblocks — that stand in the way of "the way". We recall that in Christ the way is inseparably linked with truth and life. Therefore, Christ's Gospel divides, as

3

well as unites, when it confronts our sinful deception and rebellion. The Easter victory has dethroned, but not yet destroyed, the "principalities and powers of this age" that are opposed to the coming of God's Kingdom. These still operate both outside and inside our church structures. Therefore Christ declares: "Not every one who says to me, 'Lord, Lord' shall enter the Kingdom of heaven, but the one who does the will of my Father who is in heaven."

A. Confessing the faith

In January 1982, a major advance was made on the ecumenical journey. On the authority of the World Council's Central Committee, over 100 theologians recommended unanimously to transmit an agreed statement on "Baptism, Eucharist and Ministry" to the churches for their common study and official response. These biblical scholars and doctrinal specialists, coming from over thirty countries, represented virtually all the major Christian church traditions: Eastern Orthodox, Oriental Orthodox, Roman Catholic, Old Catholic, Lutheran, Anglican, Reformed, Methodist, United, Disciples, Baptist, Adventist and Pentecostal.

Recommendation: study and reception

The Faith and Order Commission now presents this Lima text (1982) to the churches. We do so with deep conviction, for we have become increasingly aware of our unity in the body of Christ. We have found reason to rejoice in the rediscovery of the richness of our common inheritance in the Gospel. We believe that the Holy Spirit has led us to this time in the ecumenical movement when sadly divided churches have been enabled to arrive at substantial theological agreements. We believe that many significant advances are possible if in our churches we are sufficiently courageous and imaginative to embrace God's gift of Church unity.

As concrete evidence of their ecumenical commitment, the churches are being asked to enable the widest possible involvement of the whole people of God at all levels of church life in the spiritual process of receiving this text.

Behind the momentous action was over a decade of thorough preparation. It involved many consultations among scholars of various traditions on disputed areas of doctrine. It required careful consideration and coordination of the theological agreements registered in many recent dialogues between the churches and organic union negotiations among the churches. It demanded continual interchanges with church leaders and theological commissions as they critically evaluated earlier drafts of the document.

Under the guidance of the Holy Spirit, the answer to all this work and prayer was unprecedented in the modern ecumenical movement. Basic convergence was achieved on many essential parts of the apostolic faith that had formerly divided the churches and prevented them from sharing in eucharistic and conciliar fellowship together. While such theological agreements will not guarantee Church unity, they certainly can help to overcome many of the mistaken or outdated reasons frequently given to justify our disunity.

Now, how will the churches respond? Clearly they are at a major fork on the road to Church unity. Will they move forward and embody this common understanding of the apostolic faith in their dialogues, official relations and unity negotiations with other churches? Can they incorporate this sufficient agreement on the Church's Gospel and sacraments within their own practices of worship, teaching, witness and service?

More concretely, what definite steps may already now be taken to authorize the mutual recognition of our ordained ministries, the common acceptance of each other's baptism, and the joyful extension of eucharistic hospitality both among our churches and within our ecumenical gatherings? Similarly, since so many of the recent negotiations for uniting churches have lost their way on precisely these issues of ministry and sacraments, might they not now start afresh by reappropriating together their common apostolic tradition?

Or, sadly, will some churches only react defensively to this new challenge by wandering off once again on the dead-end paths of narrow isolationism? Could the fear of travelling an unfamiliar road paralyze other churches from striding ahead, especially at such a critical time when they are also confronted by internal schism and external attacks?

B. Living the Gospel

By sharing in one Lord, one faith and one baptism, the Church is also called to show forth its given unity in Christ through all that it says and does. This is to become evident in the steps taken by the churches in their common witness and service in the renewal of the "whole inhabited earth" (oikoumene), most especially in those steps taken together in solidarity with the world's poor, suffering and oppressed.

"God so loved the world..." We dare never forget — nor allow others to forget — that Christ lived in the world and died for the world. As the body of Christ in today's world, a united Church is likewise called to proclaim and serve God's Kingdom of righteousness, love and peace. It is in the world that we must witness to the signs of God's reign among us, and it is in the world that we must struggle against those evil forces that oppose the coming of God's Kingdom. This is why the churches' struggle for peace, justice and freedom is an area in need of special ecumenical self-examination. Such efforts disclose all the risks and ambiguities in taking those steps for Church unity and societal renewal that truly accord with the mind of Christ.

In the process, we Christians have frequently found ourselves in a dilemma. On the one hand, we have experienced powerful centrifugal forces in current church life. Moving out from the trinitarian centre, we have been led by the Spirit to develop doctrinal convergences in baptism, eucharist and ministry that call for more ecclesiological and theological explication of the apostolic faith, more mutual recognition and official action in the spiritual process of reception, and more reverence for the Church as God's sign and instrument for the renewal of humankind.

On the other hand, we have also experienced formidable centripetal forces that press in upon the churches from the many struggles in contemporary society. Political, economic, social and ideological movements frequently cut across confessional allegiances and theological traditions in ways that are at once destructive of consensus and yet vital for relevance and credibility. As a result, the unity and renewal of the Church and the human community take place simultaneously, in both directions, under the convulsive impact of the in-breaking reign of God who is both Head of the Church and Lord of the nations.

In such a dynamic situation, it is required that Christians persevere in their distinctive calling of enabling greater expressions of visible Church unity, and that they do so far more intentionally against the universal horizons of creation, history and culture within which the Church prefigures the end time of "…. all things under him, that God may be everything to every one" (I Cor. 15:28).

So the ecumenical journey continues. Clearly the road ahead is both promising and perilous. Commitment to the goal and determination to take steps ahead are basically a matter of obedience. To follow Christ in the pursuit of unity is to trust him even when we do not know where he is taking us. "Follow me" is a compass, not a road map. Such a journey is a test of faith, an examination of our will by the

Spirit, always an exciting adventure. "Did not our hearts burn within us while he talked to us on the road?" Whether it happens in Emmaus, Chiangmai, Budapest or Oslo, this is the universal testimony of those disciples in every time and place who have walked together with the risen Christ.

An ecumenical milestone

So that's what John was so excited about!

Bishop David was quickly flipping through the pages of the impressive 34-page document that had just arrived from Geneva in the morning mail. Well, that's probably good news, he thought, when he saw that the section on "The Eucharist" — following the opening one on "Baptism" — was far shorter than he had feared.

Here it comes, he chuckled aloud, as he reached a third section devoted to "The Ministry". His jovial expression suddenly changed, however, when he realized that this was also the last section, and longer than the previous two parts combined.

The ministry is probably still the hardest ecumenical nut to crack, the bishop lamented, as he unconsciously glanced down at his episcopal ring. Shaking his head, he remembered all the hours spent on the issue of episcopacy during their recent church union negotiations.

John Tomlinson, their seminary's top theologian, was also terribly depressed after those unsuccessful talks. And yet, he recalled, John was so elated when he returned from Lima, Peru, where he had represented their church in the latest triennial meeting of the World Council's Faith and Order Commission.

After decades of studies and consultations, John reported, the most comprehensive theological forum in the Christian Church was able to arrive at major agreements on the controversial doctrines of baptism, eucharist and ministry. It was truly an ecumenical milestone, he said. The delegates at Lima broke into spontaneous applause and corporate prayer after their unanimous vote was recorded!

The bishop smiled again, recalling the buoyant enthusiasm of the normally mild-mannered professor.

Putting aside his copy of the document, Bishop David re-read the covering letter from the General Secretary of the World Council of Churches, who also stressed that the churches have now reached a new stage in the ecumenical movement. For the first time, divided churches are being asked to act together on unifying doctrine. Specifically, they are being invited to prepare an official response to this Lima text by 1985 "at the highest appropriate level of authority". They should critically evaluate its loyalty to the faith of the apostolic Church and draw the ecumenical consequences, for their own worship and teaching as much as for their relations with other churches. Well, that will certainly give us an exciting synod meeting, the bishop thought.

In the meantime, the General Secretary continued, all churches are also being asked to familiarize their people with this material in their worship, study and witness. The Faith and Order Secretariat has been authorized to provide special resource materials for this purpose: a volume of theological essays to explain the crucial choices made by the editors of the convergence texts, and another volume of liturgical rites to help pastors and priests to put these agreements into worship practice.

That's all very good, thought Bishop David, but what about the reception by the laity? After all, we've got to arrive at a common mind of the whole people of God if we're to make any ecumencial advance.

Flipping through the pages of the text again, he slowly read aloud: "*cheirotonein ... ordo clarissimus ...* Ignatius of Antioch ... *hiereus ...* Clement of Rome ... *charism ...* epikletic." No, he said to himself, clearly some parts of this Lima material are just too technical or historical for our general readers. (I think I've forgotten the meaning of *cheirotonein* myself!)

What's really needed, thought the bishop, is a clear study guide which can be put directly into the hands of the laity. If it were really understandable, I'm sure they'd be interested. Closing his eyes to concentrate, he tried to picture what might be helpful for the Sunday morning adult education class down at St Mark's.

Yes, it should include some of the most important portions of the Lima text itself, he thought, because most of our people won't have access to the entire document. Foreign words ought to be translated and most of the historical sections eliminated. Paragraphs could be shortened and the chief ideas outlined. Pictures and illustrations would probably be helpful, along with lots of pertinent questions to spark the class discussions. Perhaps it could be designed into a flexible study course, with units devoted to each of the three major themes.

Then it hit him: and it should all be related to real problems that our people face every day in church and society! The bishop nodded his head vigorously. This was likely the key to lay reception: the text should prove its worth by tackling tough issues. For example, how about reconciling the beliefs of those Christians who baptize infants and those who don't?

11

The idea had come naturally to the bishop. In ten minutes a delegation was due from St Luke's. They had made an appointment to discuss the controversial position of their pastor, Stephen Cooke, a young man in his first parish who refused to baptize his own baby girl until she was old enough to make her own profession of faith. Never a dull moment in this diocese!

Reaching for the telephone to give Pastor Cooke some last-minute reassurance, Bishop David made a mental note to send off a letter to Faith and Order in Geneva to outline all his ideas about that lay study guide.

Personal postscript

You probably realize by now, dear reader, that you have just read a fictionalized story which outlines the background and purposes of this study guide. The facts are true but the persons are not real. There are a dozen more similar stories in this book.

In the following pages, you will find twelve study units, four each devoted to the three major themes of baptism, eucharist (Lord's Supper, holy communion) and ministry (priesthood, service). In each unit, you and your friends will be enabled to study theology in the context of daily life by considering:
1) a current challenge in church or society;
2) a theological response that is taken directly from the official ecumenical agreement document;
3) some discussion questions to assist your group to evaluate the text's loyalty and effectiveness.

When these elements properly interact, we hope you and the other study participants will experience deeper understandings, more wholesome attitudes and more responsible patterns of action with reference to the faith and life of the Christian Church today. We wish you God's blessings on your ecumenical journey!

Baptism

Confession and confusion

Discussing subjects like baptism, eucharist and ministry would be a new experience for most of them. As the adult study group of St Mark's Church got under way, four of the participants spoke up to tell how they felt about their beliefs.

"I don't know what I believe any more," Katherine said. "I grew up going to church regularly and believing everything the Bible said. And certainly I never questioned the creed. But now, I don't know. I like the idea of this study, but it will probably just make others more sure of what they believe and leave me more confused. I'm afraid I'll feel even more left out. Anyhow the eucharist gives me comfort."

Mrs Christensen knew what she believed. She wished Katherine could too. "I've just always been convinced by the Gospel and always will be, I guess. Maybe the reason why so many people have doubts is because the national church hasn't been more positive in what it teaches. It should be definite like our pastor and say, I know and am persuaded. I hope the study will just come right out and say that.''

Thompson had just recently become a baptized church member, "because I found that faith works", he said. "I decided to try going to church one day when things got out of hand for me. I don't understand the Christian teachings yet, and I'm willing to learn, but I'm not sure that matters. I just feel the church is in touch with something good and for now at least it is getting me on the right track."

Dr Ventnor said: "Sure, I believe there is a God. How else would the universe be here? But what does that have to do with the church's ministry and sacraments?" He was a successful young physician who had been baptized as an infant but had lost touch with the church and hadn't missed it. His Sundays were taken up mostly with his research on aging. His friend Thompson had persuaded him to come to the study to find out what the church is doing. He had said he would come, "if you will help me solve some of my problems at work, but you will have to show me the church isn't hopelessly out of date."

As a baptized Christian, why do you believe? Circle how much your own feelings are like those expressed by:

	Very much	Somewhat	Very little	Not at all
a) Katherine	3	2	1	0
b) Mrs Christensen	3	2	1	0
c) Thompson	3	2	1	0
d) Dr Ventnor	3	2	1	0

Baptism (1)

I. The institution of baptism

Christian baptism is rooted in the *ministry of Jesus* of Nazareth, in his death and in his resurrection. It is incorporation into Christ, who is the crucified and risen Lord; it is entry into the New Covenant between God and God's people. Baptism is a gift of God, and is administered in the name of the Father, the Son, and the Holy Spirit. St Matthew records that the risen Lord, when sending his disciples into the world, commanded them to baptize (Matt. 28:18-20).

The universal practice of baptism by the apostolic Church from its earliest days is attested in letters of the New Testament, the Acts of the Apostles, and the writings of the Fathers. The churches today continue this practice as a *rite of commitment* to the Lord who bestows his grace upon his people.

II. The meaning of baptism (1)

A. Participation in Christ's death and resurrection

Baptism means participating in the life, death and resurrection of Jesus Christ. Jesus went down into the river Jordan and was baptized in *solidarity with sinners* in order to fulfill all righteousness (Matt. 3:15). This baptism led Jesus along the way of the Suffering Servant, made manifest in his sufferings, death and resurrection (Mark 10:38-40, 45).

By baptism, Christians are immersed in the liberating death of Christ where their sins are buried, where the "old Adam" is *crucified with Christ*, and where the power of sin is broken. Thus those baptized are no longer slaves to sin, but free. Fully identified with the death of Christ, they are buried with him and raised here and now to a new *life* in the power of the resurrection of Jesus Christ, confident that they will also ultimately be one with him in a resurrection like his (Rom. 6:3-11; Col. 2:13, 3:1; Eph. 2:5-6).

17

B. Conversion, pardoning and cleansing

The baptism which makes Christians partakers of the mystery of Christ's death and resurrection implies *confession* of sin and *conversion* of heart. The baptism administered by John was itself a baptism of repentance for the forgiveness of sins (Mark 1:4).

The New Testament underlines the *ethical implications* of baptism by representing it as an ablution which washes the body with pure water, a cleansing of the heart of all sin, and an act of justification (Heb. 10:22; I Pet. 3:21; Acts 22:16; I Cor. 6:11). Thus those baptized are pardoned, cleansed and sanctified by Christ and are given as part of their baptismal experience a new ethical orientation under the guidance of the Holy Spirit.

III. Recommendation: baptismal renewal

In many large European and North American majority churches infant baptism is often practised in an apparently indiscriminate way. This contributes to the reluctance of churches which practise believers' baptism to acknowledge the validity of infant baptism; this fact should lead to more critical reflection on the meaning of baptism within those majority churches themselves.

Discussion questions

1. The early Church understood its "Great Commission" from Christ in terms of "Go... make disciples... baptize... teach..." Is that mandate still binding for the Church today? What forms of mission are most appropriate in your society?

2. Why does your church still baptize people? What does baptism achieve?

3. The Lima text, extracts from which you have been reading, aims to be faithful to "the faith of the Church throughout the ages". How much authority does your church give to: (a) scripture, (b) creeds, (c) councils, (d) confessions, (e) reason, (f) personal experience?

4. Do you believe that Christian baptism is necessary for salvation? Just what is salvation? When does it begin? Whom does it include? Where does it end?

5. All Christians are united with Christ in his life, death and resurrection through baptism. What does this say about their relation to one another? What does it say about their relation to the world in which Christ lived and for which he died?

Babel revisited

All four members of the Hughes family belong to the same Protestant congregation, but their understandings of their faith have become very different. They sometimes wonder whether they have any faith in common any more. They have all been baptized, but none of them agrees on anything important.

The wife has joined a private prayer meeting made up of people from various churches. She had heard of the deep religious experiences of the members of the group, and wanted something more spiritual for her life. She found much enthusiasm in the group and decided to go on attending. At the third meeting she heard a person speaking in tongues. This moved her so much that she now hopes she may also be able to "receive the Spirit".

The husband isn't much interested in the prayer group. He has always just gone along with the church without getting much excited about spiritual experiences or subtle points of doctrine. He is an active member of a local political organization and has close friends in it who belong

21

to other denominations and other faiths, some to no church. Occasionally he gets into discussions with them about religious matters. When he does, he finds that they all believe about the same as he does, especially about right and wrong. They all feel that the Ten Commandments are basic to religion; so he says one denomination teaches much the same as another.

The son, eighteen, has interests in a group that meditates. He says the powers of the mind have never been realized by the Western world. Though meditation is still a hobby with him, it gives him contact with some persons who follow a Buddhist philosophy. He has run into others who enjoy astrology, and still others whose main religion is nature and the outdoors. He finds that he can fit all these beliefs in with what he feels about Jesus. He sees love as the basis of all religion.

The grandmother, who lives with the family, has been a very religious person all her life. She worshipped regularly until she moved to live with her son's family. But being unacquainted now with most of the people in their congregation, she has an uneasy feeling about going to church. Instead her main interest is a religious radio programme she has listened to for twenty years. Though it is a non-denominational broadcast, she likes it because it agrees with her opinions on the country and on the Bible. She is particularly moved when the radio preacher gives testimonies on how he overcame the sin in his life when he was converted.

To what extent are Christian beliefs reflected in the Hughes family (circle)?

	Much	Somewhat	Little	Not at all
a) Wife	3	2	1	0
b) Husband	3	2	1	0
c) Son	3	2	1	0
d) Grandmother	3	2	1	0

The one whose religious faith is most like mine is _____

I cannot select any because _____

_____

Baptism (2)

I. The meaning of baptism (2)

C. The gift of the Spirit

The Holy Spirit is at work in the lives of people before, in and after their baptism. It is the same Spirit who revealed Jesus as the Son (Mark 1:10-11) and who empowered and united the disciples at Pentecost (Acts 2). God bestows upon all baptized persons the anointing and the promise of the Holy Spirit, marks them with a seal and implants in their hearts the first instalment of their inheritance as sons and daughters of God. The Holy Spirit nurtures the *life of faith* when they will enter into its full possession, to the praise of the glory of God (II Cor. 1:21-22; Eph. 1:13-14).

D. Incorporation into the body of Christ

Administered in obedience to our Lord, baptism is a *sign and seal* of our common discipleship. Through baptism, Christians are brought into union with Christ, with each other and with the Church of every time and place. Our common baptism, which unites us to Christ in faith, is thus a basic bond of unity. We are one people and are called to confess and serve one Lord in each place and in all the world. The union with Christ which we share through baptism has important implications for Christian unity. "There is... one baptism, one God and Father of us all..." (Eph. 4:4-6).

When baptismal unity is realized in one holy, catholic, apostolic Church, a genuine Christian witness can be made to the healing and reconciling love of God. Therefore, our one baptism into Christ constitutes a call to the churches to *overcome their divisions* and visibly manifest their fellowship.

The inability of the churches mutually to recognize their various practices of baptism as sharing in the one baptism, and their actual dividedness in spite of mutual baptismal recognition, have given dramatic visibility to the *broken witness* of the Church. The readiness of the churches in some places and times to allow differences of sex, race, or social status to divide the body of Christ has further called into question genuine baptismal unity of the Christian community (Gal. 3:27-28) and has seriously compromised its witness.

The need to *recover baptismal unity* is at the heart of the ecumenical task as it is central for the realization of genuine partnership within the Christian communities.

E. The sign of the Kingdom

Baptism *initiates* the reality of the new life given in the midst of the present world. It gives participation in the community of the Holy Spirit. It is a sign of the Kingdom of God and of the life of the world to come. Through the gifts of faith, hope and love, baptism has a dynamic which embraces the whole of life, extends to all nations, and *anticipates* the day when every tongue will confess that Jesus Christ is Lord to the glory of God the Father.

II. Recommendation: mutual recognition of baptism

Churches are increasingly recognizing each other's baptism as the one baptism into Christ when Jesus Christ has been confessed as Lord by the candidate or, in the case of infant baptism, when confession has been made by the church (parents, guardians, godparents and congregation) and affirmed later by personal faith and commitment. *Mutual recognition* of baptism is acknowledged as an important sign and means of expressing the baptismal unity given in Christ. Wherever possible, mutual recognition should be expressed explicitly by the churches.

Discussion questions

1. Have you ever attended a baptism in another church? How did it compare with the celebration of baptism in your church in terms of its wording, participants and setting?

2. What is the importance of baptism for Christian unity? Into which church is a person baptized? Is there more than one Church?

3. In ecumenical discussions we frequently use the phrase "unity in diversity". Where does unity end and uniformity begin? When does diversity degenerate into division?

4. What are the controversies you have come across on the subject of baptism? What position does your church take on these?

5. We confess that the Holy Spirit incorporates baptized persons into the body of Christ, a Church that is "one, holy, catholic and apostolic". What does that say about our present divisions, conformity to the world, individualism and religious factions?

Christians: old and new

Maria's blue jeans seemed strangely incongruous with her long braided hair. Yet mixing the modern with the traditional was not at all unusual for her. It was a characteristic that made her a constant delight to her fellow students at the university. They were never quite sure whether she was going to quote someone like Dostoevsky or Brecht, to say nothing of humming aloud from both "rock" music and the Orthodox liturgy. In her religious life, however, Maria experienced an inner turmoil that she rarely shared with others. Even her closest friend, Tanya, could not really understand or approve of her increasingly frequent visits to the small congregation of "New Christians" in town.

"Our people have been Orthodox for centuries and centuries," Tanya insisted. "You are still a loyal Christian, Maria. You love the Lord. If not everything is to your liking in our church, stay and help us change it gradually from the inside. Nothing will be gained by leaving!"

Maria respected Tanya, but she remained impatient and unconvinced. There had been no organized parishes near her home as a child. She therefore joined with her parents in closely following the liturgical life of a local monastic community. As the years passed, though, she became growingly dissatisfied with the community's traditional routine. There seemed too few opportunities for personal involvement, and so little sensitivity for parish renewal and modern development.

"I'm sure that the Orthodox faith is eternally true," she would say quietly to Tanya, "but it's so hard for me to understand how to put it all into everyday practice."

It was only after she started to attend the university that Maria became attracted to the congregations of "New Christians". She liked their modern music, free prayers, and the fuller participation of lay persons in Sunday worship. The adult discussions in Christian education were also lively. Though she had to admit that she certainly missed the awesome beauty of the Orthodox liturgy, she really did feel closer to daily life in her new church home. That is, until the pastor began to talk privately to her about being rebaptized — as a reborn Christian.

The leader of the congregation explained that her baptism as an infant in that remote Orthodox monastery was of no real effect. Why? Because her Christian faith was never personally and publicly expressed. Her baptism was not actually a sign of Christian conversion. It was more like a family presentation in the temple according to the social customs of the traditionally Orthodox people.

No, the pastor said, if Maria wanted to continue in this community church, and she was certainly very welcome, then she would be expected to make a public profession of the faith and be baptized in the Spirit.

"But I'm already baptized in the Spirit!" was Maria's spontaneous response. It was on that basis that she had been a faithful member of the Orthodox Church for over twenty years.

30

She could understand and even accept some variety of baptismal rites in the various churches. Indeed, didn't her own personal experience demonstrate the weakness in baptizing all infants of Christian parents and then not providing enough care later for their nurture in Christian education and service? Yet Maria could not bring herself to believe that she must now reject her baptism as an infant, in order to become more fully engaged in active Christian discipleship.

For months now, Maria did not know which way to turn. She wanted desperately to become part of church renewal. But she could not see why some Christian communities wanted to increase their membership by denying the infant baptism of other churches in the same place. She was completely stupified when she also learned from Tanya that both churches were members together in the World Council of Churches.

Baptism (3)

I. Baptism of believers and infants

While the possibility that infant baptism was also practised in the apostolic age cannot be excluded, baptism upon
personal profession of faith is the most clearly attested pattern in the New Testament documents.

In the course of history, the practice of baptism has
developed in a *variety of forms*. Some churches baptize *infants* brought by parents or guardians who are ready, in and
with the Church, to bring up the children in the Christian
faith. Other churches practise exclusively the baptism of
believers who are able to make a personal confession of
faith. Some of these churches encourage infants or children
to be presented and blessed in a service which usually involves thanksgiving for the gift of the child and also the
commitment of the mother and father to Christian parent-
hood. All churches baptize believers coming from other
religions or from unbelief who accept the Christian faith
and participate in catechetical instruction.

Both the baptism of believers and the baptism of infants
take place *in the Church* as the community of faith. When
one who can answer for himself or herself is baptized, a personal confession of faith will be an integral part of the baptismal service. When an infant is baptized, the personal
response will be offered at a later moment in life.

In both cases, the baptized person will have *to grow* in the
understanding of faith. For those baptized upon their own
confession of faith, there is always the constant requirement
of a continuing growth of personal response in faith. In the
case of infants, personal confession is expected later, and
Christian nurture is directed to the eliciting of this confession.

All baptism is rooted in and declares Christ's faithfulness
unto death. It has its *setting* within the life and faith of the
Church and, through the witness of the whole Church,
points to the faithfulness of God, the ground of all life in
faith. At every baptism the whole congregation reaffirms its

faith in God and pledges itself to provide an environment of witness and service. Baptism should, therefore, always be celebrated and developed in the setting of the Christian community.

Both forms of baptism require a similar and responsible attitude towards *Christian nurture*. A rediscovery of the continuing character of Christian nurture may facilitate the mutual acceptance of different initiation practices.

In order to overcome their differences, believer baptists and those who practise infant baptism should *reconsider* certain aspects of their practices. The *first* may seek to express more visibly the fact that children are placed under the protection of God's grace. The *latter* must guard themselves against the practice of apparently indiscriminate baptism and take more seriously their responsibility for the nurture of baptized children to mature commitment to Christ.

II. Recommendation: no "re-baptism"

Baptism is an *unrepeatable* act. Any practice which might be interpreted as "re-baptism" must be avoided.

As the churches come to fuller mutual understanding and acceptance of one another and enter into closer relationships in witness and service, they will want to refrain from any practice which might call into question the *sacramental integrity* of the other churches or which might diminish the unrepeatability of the sacrament of baptism.

Discussion questions

1. What are the main differences between the approaches of those who favour infant baptism and those who advocate believers' baptism?

2. Both groups make positive affirmations. Do these complement or contradict each other?

3. In some churches it has been possible to regard as "equivalent alternatives" for entry into the Church both (a) a pattern whereby baptism in infancy is followed by later profession of faith, and (b) a pattern whereby believers' baptism follows upon a presentation and blessing in infancy. Could your church recognize such "equivalent alternatives" in its reciprocal relationships and in church union negotiations?

4. "We acknowledge one baptism for the forgiveness of sins" (Nicene Creed). Is it defensible in either scripture or tradition to separate two baptisms, one in water and the other in the Spirit? How do you explain the personal experience of Philip and Cornelius (Acts 8,10) in view of the baptismal theology of the apostolic Church (cf. Rom. 6:4-6; I Cor. 12:12-13; Eph. 4:4-6)?

5. Is baptism merely a private rite in the church of the past? What would change if we could rather see ourselves as baptized into a communal style of life for the world in the present?

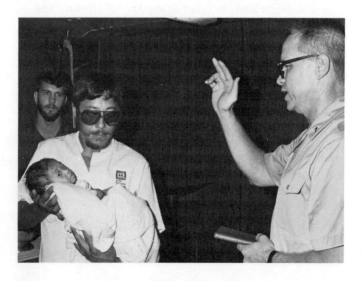

God in our image

The taxi lurched to a sudden halt. Canon Peter Milton had arrived at the home of Joseph Nsimba. Sooner than he had expected. "Africanization" was the subject he came to discuss with this retired pastor of sixty years' service. The memories of such veteran church leaders were providing his colleagues at church headquarters with invaluable data.

Here are a few of the highlights recorded by Milton during the next few hours of their probing conversation:

Milton: What is the relation between church sacraments and African culture? What are some of the theological and pastoral issues which still need more attention?

Nsimba: Baptism and holy communion vividly convey the meaning of the person of Christ as well as his saving work.

During the missionary era, however, the reality of Christ was often confused with the forms of Western culture. Christ was domesticated. He was proclaimed only in the context of Western categories and symbols. These were seen as being superior to the indigenous and so-called "pagan" cultures of Africa. The teachings and practices of the missionaries frequently carried with them the economic, political, and ethical systems and values of Western cultures.

Milton: Would you please cite some examples?

Nsimba: In many churches, Africans were told to take "Christian" names. Only after the Bible was translated in our own language did we realize that the names of many missionaries, such as Martin, Leon, Harvey, Olivier and Dorothee, were not in the Bible. We also learned that Saint Augustine, Saint Ambrose and many other Western theologians did not have Christian names. Furthermore, most astonishing of all, Jesus did not invent a Christian name for himself. He was given a name which derived from the Hebrew verb that means "to save". By this name God honoured the Chosen People and their culture and revealed to them in person the true meaning of salvation.

In my Congo culture, a name was given to the child six days after birth. That name performed many functions. It was used, for example, for ritualistic protection against evil powers. By somebody's name, one could often guess the history of the individual or the family and tribe to which she or he belonged. But the missionaries didn't believe that such African names could also be used at the time of baptism.

Milton: How about local practices in holy communion?

Nsimba: The sole use of bread and wine — foods unknown to the diet of many Africans — was identified not only with the missionary's foreign economy but also with the white people's sorcery and witchcraft. Some African Christians refused to commune because it was believed that the white people's bread and wine used in the eucharist were the flesh and blood of men and women whom the missionaries had killed by their sorcery. Taking part in holy communion was therefore viewed by some as an initiation rite into the social evil most feared in the native community.

Now, as for polygamy...

Baptism (4)

I. The celebration of baptism

Baptism is *administered* with water in the name of the Father, the Son and the Holy Spirit.

In the celebration of baptism the symbolic dimension of water should be taken seriously and not minimalized. The act of *immersion* can vividly express the reality that in baptism the Christian participates in the death, burial and resurrection of Christ.

As seen in some theological traditions, the use of water, with all its *positive* associations with life and blessing, signifies the continuity between the old and the new creation, thus revealing the significance of baptism not only for human beings but also for the whole cosmos. At the same time, the use of water represents a purification of creation, a dying to that which is negative and destructive in the world: those who are baptized into the body of Christ are made partakers of a renewed existence.

As was the case in the early centuries, the gift of the Spirit in baptism may be signified in additional ways; for example, by the sign of the *laying on of hands*, and by anointing or *chrismation*. The very *sign of the cross* recalls the promised gift of the Holy Spirit who is the instalment and pledge of what is yet to come when God has fully redeemed those whom he has made his own (Eph. 1:13-14). The recovery of such vivid signs may be expected to enrich the liturgy.

Within any comprehensive *order of baptism* at least the following elements should find a place: the proclamation of the scriptures referring to baptism; an invocation of the Holy Spirit; a renunciation of evil; a profession of faith in Christ and the Holy Trinity; the use of water; a declaration that the persons baptized have acquired a new identity as sons and daughters of God, and as members of the Church, called to be witnesses of the Gospel. Some churches consider that Christian initiation is not complete without the

39

sealing of the baptized with the gift of the Holy Spirit and participation in holy communion.

It is appropriate to explain in the context of the baptismal service the *meaning* of baptism as it appears from scriptures (i.e. the participation in Christ's death and resurrection, conversion, pardoning and cleansing, gift of the Spirit, incorporation into the body of Christ, and sign of the Kingdom).

Since baptism is intimately connected with the corporate life and worship of the Church, it should normally be administered during *public worship*, so that the members of the congregation may be reminded of their own baptism and may welcome into their fellowship those who are baptized and whom they are committed to nurture in the Christian faith. The sacrament is appropriate to great festival occasions such as Easter, Pentecost and Epiphany, as was the practice in the early Church.

II. Recommendation: baptismal identity

In some parts of the world, the *giving of a name* in the baptismal liturgy has led to confusion between baptism and customs surrounding name-giving. This confusion is especially harmful if, in cultures predominantly not Christian, the baptized are required to assume Christian names not rooted in their cultural tradition.

In making regulations for baptism, churches should be careful to keep the emphasis on the true *Christian significance* of baptism and to avoid unnecessarily alienating the baptized from their local culture through the imposition of foreign names. A name which is inherited from one's original culture roots the baptized in that culture, and at the same time manifests the universality of baptism, incorporation into the one Church, holy, catholic and apostolic, which stretches over all the nations of the earth.

Discussion questions

1. How much cultural diversity is compatible with Christian unity?

2. Paul affirmed that any one baptized in Christ is a new creation: "the old has passed away, behold, the new has come". How do we live out our new identity in Christ amid our persisting societal identifications (sex, race, nation) among other persons also created in God's image?

3. The relation of Jesus Christ to history and culture has been variously answered in the life of the church in different parts of the world. What should happen when Christ and the Christian church encounter powerful forces and traditional loyalties within our historical and cultural traditions?

4. How do you view the relation of Christianity to other living faiths and ideological commitments? What lessons can the churches learn from their missionary activities in previous generations?

5. How have you found it best to witness to the Christian faith with your friends and associates? Which gifts of the Holy Spirit are most helpful in such encounters?

Eucharist

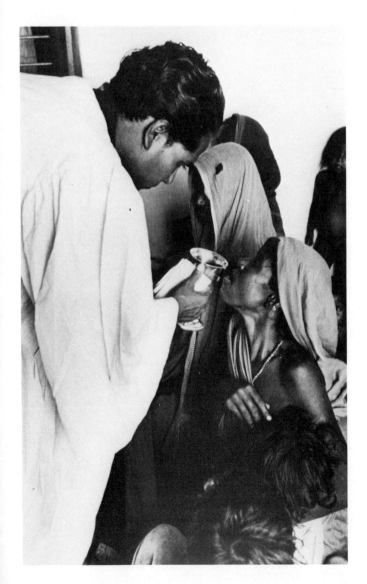

Sunday and Monday worlds

The Bells grew up in the church, always liked it, and like it more each passing year. Most of their friends belong there. They go to a Wednesday evening prayer group and work with a youth group which is interested in the supernatural and decisions for Jesus. In a way the Bells look forward to death because, to them, life after death is the only thing that makes sense of life here and now. They believe God created the world, but he works in it now just to save it and not to start anything new.

They do have jobs, buy groceries, and keep their house in good repair; but they don't go in much for politics, for world news, or even for all the concern over ecology and energy. Those are mostly matters of the world, they say; the spirit world beyond is what counts. The eucharist reminds them how much even Jesus had to suffer here on earth.

Fran and Russ Woods also grew up in the church and enjoyed it up through their last year in high school, but then something changed. They began to question its beliefs and distrust its purpose. So many of their questions were being answered outside the church. For them, disease was cured by science, not religion; entertainment was found in television, not a church group; food production was increased by research, not prayers.

The Woods seldom go to church any more, and they are disappointed when they do. Instead they feel they are doing more as members of a community organization which has cleaned up a stream near their home, campaigned for medical research, and improved the laboratory of their high school.

They believe there is a God, but they think of him most when they vacation at the lakes. They try not to think of him when they visit their uncle who has cancer, because they have doubts about a God who would allow such suffering. Religious idealists usually get crucified. They believe the problems of the world can best be solved by getting to work on them here and now.

Joel and Jenny Johnson live in both a Sunday world and a Monday world. Most Sundays they go to church and enjoy going. They find their favourite hymns there, and their favourite friends. Holy communion means much to them, and so does Easter. They find strength in the forgiveness of sins and the resurrection. They believe in Christ.

On Mondays Joel is the managing accountant for a small plant, and Jenny teaches biology. Jenny is a member of the teachers' union, and Joel represents his office at political functions. They have a full life, but they also have their problems.

One of their problems is getting their Sunday world and Monday world together. They know they should be witnessing to their Monday friends about God, but when they do, they can't find Monday words to explain redemption so they just end up inviting them to Sunday church.

When politics or business comes up at church, Joel is uneasy because he is afraid the preacher won't know the facts of life. When death and suffering come up in biology class, Jenny is uneasy because she has a hard time understanding why God lets it go on. What she teaches in biology seems out of place in church school and what she teaches in church school seems out of place in biology.

When the Johnsons read the papers, they are even more perplexed. They can see little connection between what the church paper says on Sunday and what the city paper says on Monday. Now and then they give a cheque to help some earthquake victims, but if the Prime Minister doesn't bring peace, it won't be brought, and if government doesn't solve the shortages, they won't be solved.

The Johnsons would like to get their two worlds together, but they can't find the link. Can you?

Eucharist (1)

I. The institution of the eucharist

The Church receives the eucharist as *a gift* from the Lord. St Paul wrote: "I have received from the Lord what I also delivered to you, that the Lord Jesus on the night when he was betrayed took bread, and when he had given thanks, he broke it, and said: 'This is my body, which is for you. Do this in remembrance (*anamnesis*) of me.' In the same way also the cup, after supper, saying: 'This cup is the new covenant in my blood. Do this, as often as you drink it, in remembrance of me.' " (I Cor. 11:23-25; cf. Matt. 26:26-29; Mark 14:22-25; Luke 22:14-20).

The eucharist is a sacramental meal which by visible signs communicates to us God's love in Jesus Christ, the love by which Jesus loved his own "to the end" (John 13:1). It has acquired many names: for example, the Lord's Supper, the breaking of bread, the holy communion, the divine liturgy, the mass. Its celebration continues as the central act of the Church's worship.

Since the memorial of Christ is the very content of the preached Word as it is of the eucharistic meal, each reinforces the other. The celebration of the eucharist properly includes the proclamation of the Word.

II. The meaning of the eucharist (1)

The eucharist is essentially the sacrament of the gift which God makes to us in Christ through the power of the Holy Spirit. Every Christian receives this gift of salvation through communion in the body and blood of Christ. In the eucharistic meal, in the eating and drinking of the bread and wine, Christ grants communion with himself. God himself acts, giving life to the body of Christ and renewing each member. In accordance with Christ's promise, each baptized member of the body of Christ receives in the eucharist the *assurance* of the forgiveness of sins (Matt. 26:28) and the *pledge* of eternal life (John 6:51-58).

49

A. Thanksgiving to the Father

The eucharist, which always includes both word and sacrament, is a proclamation and a celebration of the *work of God*. It is the great thanksgiving to the Father for everything accomplished in creation, redemption and sanctification, for everything which is accomplished now by God in the Church and in the world in spite of the sins of human beings, for everything that God will accomplish in bringing the Kingdom to fulfilment. Thus the eucharist is the benediction (*berakah*) by which the Church expresses its thankfulness for all God's benefits.

The eucharist is the great *sacrifice of praise* by which the Church speaks on behalf of the whole creation. For the world which God has reconciled is present at every eucharist: in the bread and wine, in the persons of the faithful, and in the prayers they offer for themselves and for all people. Christ unites the faithful with himself and includes their prayers within his own intercession so that the faithful are transfigured and their prayers accepted.

This sacrifice of praise is possible only through Christ, with him and in him. The bread and wine, fruits of the earth and of human labour, are presented to the Father in faith and thanksgiving. The eucharist thus signifies *what the world is to become*: an offering and hymn of praise to the Creator, a universal communion in the body of Christ, a kingdom of justice, love and peace in the Holy Spirit.

B. Meal of the Kingdom

The eucharist opens up the vision of the divine rule which has been promised as the final *renewal of creation*, and is a foretaste of it. Signs of this renewal are present in the world wherever the grace of God is manifest and human beings work for justice, love and peace. The eucharist is the feast at which the Church gives thanks to God for these signs and joyfully celebrates and anticipates the coming of the Kingdom in Christ (I Cor. 11:26; Matt. 26:29).

The very celebration of the eucharist is an instance of the Church's participation in *God's mission* to the world. This participation takes everyday form in the proclamation of the Gospel, service of the neighbour, and faithful presence in the world.

III. Recommendation: eucharistic renewal

Christian *faith is deepened* by the celebration of the Lord's Supper. Hence the eucharist should be celebrated frequently. Many differences of theology, liturgy and practice are connected with the varying frequency with which the holy communion is celebrated.

As the eucharist celebrates the resurrection of Christ, it is appropriate that it should take place *at least every Sunday*. As it is the new sacramental meal of the people of God, every Christian should be encouraged to receive communion frequently.

Discussion questions

1. The Church confesses that Jesus Christ reveals God's suffering and victorious love in his cross and resurrection. In what ways is the Church called to express its thankfulness for all God's blessings?

2. How does the eucharist convey God's personal assurance of the forgiveness of sin and the pledge of eternal life? Does frequent communion serve to strengthen your trust in God's unqualified love in Jesus Christ?

3. Our sacrifice of praise is at the heart of the eucharist. What is the role of the risen Christ in this celebration? How is this expressed during the worship service?

4. Is your ultimate hope grounded in the renewal of creation through God's mission to the world? What does it mean for the whole creation to be presented to the Creator in Christ through the Spirit? How does this trinitarian drama make the weekly celebration of the eucharist "the central act of the Church's worship"?

5. In the mystery of his person and work, Jesus Christ unites divinity and humanity, eternity and history. How can a "eucharistic lifestyle" of dying and rising with Christ help to integrate our Sunday worship and Monday work?

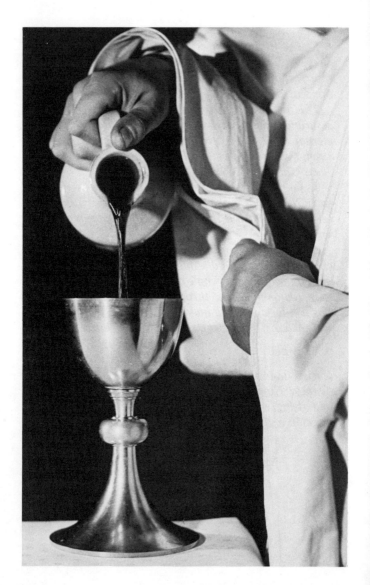

Divided at the altar

Robert looked sad at the breakfast table as his wife and children left to attend mass without him. Certainly it had not been an easy decision for him to make. He simply was no longer able to participate throughout the entire liturgy, knowing that at the end he would not be allowed to take communion with his family anyhow. And why? Because he belonged to the same Reformed Church in which he had worshipped since his childhood.

His thoughts went back over the years to their wedding. Coming from different church backgrounds, Marguerite and he had talked a lot about their faith before they decided to marry. As a devout Roman Catholic, she naturally wanted the celebration to take place in her home parish. He agreed and was very grateful when Fr Martin had especially invited the pastor of the neighbouring Reformed congregation to participate in the ceremony. How happy all their relatives had been to be able to praise God in the same church celebration! Both Marguerite and he had prayed that the two of them would soon be able to commune together on a regular basis. Their hopes were strengthened by all the ecumenical progress made during those same years at the Second Vatican Council. Pope John XXIII kept smiling at them daily from his picture hanging in their hallway.

At the first holy communion of their son Charles, however, Robert could not go to the Lord's Table. The experience of their family divided at the altar had been so painful to him that at the first holy communion of their daughter Monique in another parish, Robert resolutely advanced towards the altar. While he was not refused the sacrament, the priest afterwards explained his church's official teachings in a kind but firm way.

It was also made clear to the family that Marguerite and the children could not commune in Robert's congregation. Its holy communion could not be recognized as a full eucharist, the priest said, since it was administered by Reformed pastors who had never been ordained by Catholic bishops.

Now to be fair, Robert had to admit to himself that none of this came as a surprise. Fr Martin had already explained it fully before they were married. Nevertheless, as the years passed, he and Marguerite found it increasingly difficult to accept the impossibility of communing together in each other's churches. They were certainly no theologians but they believed essentially the same things about the eucharist. Indeed, hadn't the Second Vatican Council declared that the eucharist in the Reformed Church celebrated the memorial of the death and resurrection of the Lord? Why couldn't Marguerite commune there simply by believing what the Council affirmed, even if she were also convinced of the fullness of the Catholic eucharist? And if the Council could accept his Christian baptism within the Reformed Church as authentic, what necessarily prevented his participation at holy communion?

After quickly swallowing the last mouthful of coffee that had long since gone cold, Robert hurried through the hallway to drive down to his church — alone. In his haste, he did not even notice the smiling face of Pope John XXIII in the picture on the wall.

Eucharist (2)

I. The meaning of the eucharist (2)

C. Memorial of Christ

The eucharist is the memorial of the crucified and risen Christ, i.e. the living and effective sign of his sacrifice, accomplished once and for all on the cross and still operative on behalf of all humankind. The biblical ideal of memorial (*anamnesis*) as applied to the eucharist refers to this *present efficacy* of God's work when it is celebrated by God's people in a liturgy.

Christ himself with all that he has accomplished for us and for all creation (in his incarnation, servanthood, ministry, teaching, suffering, sacrifice, resurrection, ascension and sending of the Spirit) is present in this memorial, granting us *communion* with himself. The eucharist is also the *foretaste* of his parousia and of the final Kingdom.

The memorial in which Christ acts through the joyful celebration of his Church is thus both representation and anticipation. It is not only a calling to mind of what is past and of its significance. It is the Church's *effective* proclamation of God's mighty acts and promises.

Representation and anticipation are expressed in thanksgiving and intercession. The Church, gratefully recalling God's mighty acts of redemption, beseeches God to give the benefits of these acts to every human being.

In thanksgiving and intercession, the Church is united with the Son, its great High Priest and Intercessor (Rom. 8:34; Heb. 7:25). The eucharist is the sacrament of the *unique sacrifice* of Christ, who ever lives to make intercession for us. It is the memorial of all that God has done for the salvation of the world. What it was God's will to accomplish in the incarnation, life, death, resurrection and ascension of Christ, God does not repeat. These events are unique and can neither be repeated nor prolonged. In the memorial of the eucharist, however, the Church offers its *intercession* in communion with Christ, our great High Priest.

II. Recommendation: eucharistic sacrifice

It is in the light of the significance of the eucharist as intercession that references to the eucharist in Catholic theology as "propitiatory sacrifice" may be understood. The understanding is that there is only one expiation, that of the unique sacrifice of the cross, made actual in the eucharist and presented before the Father in the intercession of Christ and of the Church for all humanity.

In the light of the biblical conception of memorial (*anamnesis*), all churches might want to review the old controversies about "sacrifice" and deepen their understanding of the reasons why other traditions than their own have either used or rejected this term.

Discussion questions

1. The opening story is especially relevant in regions where mixed marriages are becoming more and more common. Is this true of your community? How do the churches try to minister faithfully in meeting such difficult pastoral problems?

2. Tensions arise inevitably when the Church as a personal communion is obligated to exercise discipline as an ecclesiastical organization. Think of Paul in Corinth! How should the Church reconcile the relative claims of life, love and law within its changing structures and policies?

3. In the history of the Church there have been various attempts to understand the mystery of the real and unique presence of Christ in the eucharist. Which interpretation has been most common in your tradition? In what ways was that formulation historically conditioned by current church polemics?

4. Why does the Lima text place so much emphasis on "the biblical conception of 'memorial'"? Is the risen Lord bound by our human limits of time and space in the eucharist?

5. On the basis of the gospel, are we now able to affirm ecumenically both (a) "the unique sacrifice of Christ" that can "neither be repeated nor prolonged", and (b) the eucharistic "intercession of Christ and the Church for all humanity"?

Back in tune

Some neighbourhood teenagers had been using Christ Church as a gathering place during the week and occasionally on Sundays. But their dress and their ways were distressing to the older members. In Christian hospitality, the members decided not to throw the youth out; but in honesty, they gave plenty of signs that the youth were not wanted.

Mrs McManus, the leader of the adult choir, had hoped even more than the others that the young people would leave. Her conscience bothered her a good deal, but she just could not bear seeing them pound on the grand piano she had given in memory of her mother. If only they would find some other place and leave the parish in peace!

One Sunday, the congregation celebrated the eucharist together after Father Grimes had preached on the text "God was in Christ, reconciling the world to himself, not counting their trespasses against them, and entrusted to us the message of reconciliation." Mrs McManus felt very deeply involved in both the sermon and the meal. She believed every word when the priest declared: "Given for you... shed for you."

Afterwards, Mrs McManus approached Jack Quinn, one of the most aggressive of the youth, at the water fountain. Some of the other choir members feared for what was coming. But it didn't happen. Instead she said kindly: "Jack, I like that wrist watch you are wearing." She asked him where he had got it.

Jack was completely disarmed, because the watch had belonged to his father whose memory he cherished, and it meant much to him. Through that watch the woman had complemented him on his family taste. In passing, she also mentioned her mother and the piano. One subject led to another, and before long he started asking about music and she shared the little she knew about cricket. The choir members were amazed.

Reconciliation among people comes from (circle):

		Very much	Some	Little	Not at all
a)	Basic human goodness	3	2	1	0
b)	Need to solve problems	3	2	1	0
c)	Wanting God's favour	3	2	1	0
d)	Reflecting God's forgiveness	3	2	1	0
e)	God working in us	3	2	1	0
f)	Other	3	2	1	0

Eucharist (3)

I. The meaning of the eucharist (3)

D. Invocation of the Spirit

The *words and acts of Christ* at the institution of the eucharist stand at the heart of the celebration; the eucharistic meal is the sacrament of the body and blood of Christ, the sacrament of his real presence. Christ fulfills in a variety of ways his promise to be always with his own even to the end of the world. But Christ's mode of presence in the eucharist is unique.

Jesus said over the bread and wine of the eucharist: "This is my body... this is my blood..." What Christ declared is true, and this truth is fulfilled every time the eucharist is celebrated. The Church confesses Christ's real, loving and active presence in the eucharist. While Christ's *real presence* in the eucharist does not depend on the faith of the individual, all agree that to discern the body and blood of Christ, faith is required.

The Spirit makes the crucified and risen Christ really present to us in the eucharistic meal, fulfilling the promise contained in the words of institution. The presence of Christ is clearly the centre of the eucharist, and the promise contained in the words of institution is therefore fundamental to the celebration. Yet it is the *Father* who is the primary origin and final fulfilment of the eucharistic event. The incarnate *Son of God* by and in whom it is accomplished is its living centre. The *Holy Spirit* is the immeasurable strength of love which makes it possible and continues to make it effective.

The bond between the eucharistic celebration and the mystery of the triune God reveals the *role of the Holy Spirit* as that of the One who makes the historical words of Jesus present and alive. Being assured by Jesus' promises in the words of institution that it will be answered, the Church prays to the Father for the gift of the Holy Spirit *(epiklesis)* in order that the eucharistic event may be a reality: the real presence of the crucified and risen Christ giving his life for all humanity.

It is in virtue of the living word of Christ and by the power of the Holy Spirit that the bread and wine become the sacramental *signs* of body and blood. They remain so for the purpose of communion.

The whole action of the eucharist has an invocational character because it depends upon the work of the Holy Spirit. In the words of the liturgy, this aspect of the eucharist finds varied expression. The Church, as the community of the new covenant, confidently *invokes the Spirit*, in order that it may be sanctified and renewed, led into all justice, truth and unity, and empowered to fulfill its mission in the world.

II. Recommendation: eucharistic communion

The increased mutual understanding expressed in the present statement may allow some churches to attain a greater measure of *eucharistic communion* among themselves and so bring closer the day when Christ's divided people will be visibly reunited around the Lord's Table.

Discussion questions

1. Why is the gospel of reconciliation so prominent in the New Testament? Who is the subject and who is the object of the reconciliation that centres in Jesus Christ?

2. What is unique about Christ's presence in the eucharist? Why is faith necessary to discern that real presence?

3. How does the Lima understanding of Christ's real presence in the sacrament affirm the indissoluble union between God the Son and God the Spirit? Is the invocation of the Holy Spirit an essential part of your church's liturgy?

4. The liturgical reform movement has brought the churches closer together in the manner of celebrating the Lord's Supper. Since a common eucharistic faith does not imply uniformity in either liturgy or practice, what forms of diversity do you find most helpful to your own spiritual nurture?

5. Some churches have claimed that sharing in the eucharist is the "goal" of Christian unity in the apostolic faith. Others have held that this is a "means" of achieving it. How may the tension between the "already" and the "not yet" qualities of our life in Christ guide the communion practices of churches embarked on the ecumenical pilgrimage?

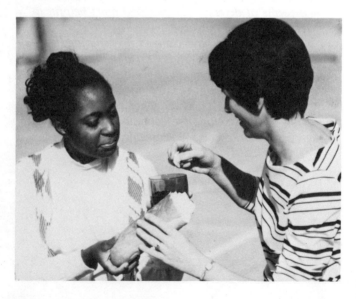

Breaking bread together

He trembled... and felt a strange sensation in his body. The congregation sang "Amen" at the end of the hymn and communion was about to begin. A few minutes earlier a deacon was called forward by the pastor in order to help distribute the elements. When he turned to face the congregation, Braulio was shocked to discover that the deacon was also his ex-boss, Don Lorenzo. Beads of sweat broke out on Braulio's forehead. His heartbeat quickened and his hands grew tense. Unable to concentrate, he barely heard the pastor reading: "Take, eat; this is my body... Do this in remembrance of me..." What should he do?

For Braulio the story was not simple. He was only two years old when his family was obliged to leave their small hut in the countryside. Like tens of thousands of others, they emigrated to the city and ended up in the slums. They paid no taxes, but neither did they enjoy any civil rights or services, like water, gas and electricity.

Braulio grew up on the streets in the midst of the masses struggling to survive. Poverty, hunger and disease were everywhere. With little incentive and some bad company, he finally ended up in prison. Convicted of theft, he was sentenced to a six-year term. But something totally unexpected happened to him in the prison.

A few of Braulio's cellmates usually went out once a week to attend some kind of meeting. Attracted by this "privilege", he asked what it was all about. One of his companions told him that a pastor conducted Bible studies with them and brought them new hope. Fed up with no visitors and always seeing the same people, Braulio asked one day for permission to go along.

The first meeting was not at all extraordinary; he didn't understand anything the pastor was talking about. But at least it was a change. It was only after some time that Braulio discovered something different and experienced what the pastor and the group would describe as "his conversion". Jesus Christ began to have central importance in his life.

After finishing his prison sentence, reduced for good behaviour, Braulio moved to his new community and began to worship in a small church located close to where he lived. On the second Sunday he was presented to the congregation, and during that same week he received the visit of a Christian brother with news about where he could find some work.

It turned out to be a small plant manufacturing spare parts for motors. Ten workers were employed there. Don Lorenzo had told him: the situation is risky, but if you like, you can start tomorrow. Braulio jumped at the chance and the next day, at seven in the morning, he began to learn how to handle a lathe.

Most of the workers were Roman Catholics, as he learned one day, when they were talking about their boss being "one of those Protestants". When asked, Braulio cautiously identified himself as belonging to the same group.

After a short while, the inflation crisis also hit their small factory. Don Lorenzo assembled his eleven workers and told them that he could no longer afford to employ them all. Six of them would have to be dismissed in order for the rest to be allowed to go on working. The bank was cutting off all credit; he either paid his debts or went bankrupt.

The workers' reaction was not long in coming. They didn't want to leave their families without support. They pledged to fight together. Their trade union backed their plan to occupy the plant. Don Lorenzo expressed his opposition, and Braulio remembered the boss's stinging words addressed to him: "Is this the thanks I get for helping you out? Do you want to go to prison that badly?"

Nevertheless the workers went ahead with their plan. They moved into the plant, slept in close quarters on the floor, and shared common meals from the little food brought to them irregularly by family members and friends. They felt closely united in a common cause as never before.

One night, after they ate their soup and broke some bread together, Braulio dared to read the Bible to the small group. Afterwards they prayed to God for help in this difficult situation.

Braulio asked his comrades to allow him to go to church on Sunday, and now... there he was, sitting on a bench in the congregation and not knowing whether to share in the eucharist.

When the pastor passed the communion bread to Don Lorenzo to distribute among the members, he saw that the deacon's eyes were filled with tears. Don Lorenzo had just discovered Braulio seated in the congregation! He felt a strange sensation in his body, he trembled...

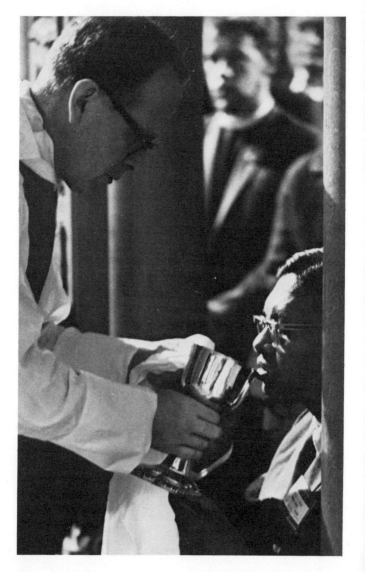

Eucharist (4)

I. The meaning of the eucharist (4)

E. Communion of the faithful

The eucharistic communion with *Christ* present, who nourishes the life of the Church, is at the same time communion within the body of Christ which is the *Church*. The sharing in one bread and the common cup in a given place demonstrates and effects the oneness of the sharers with Christ and with their fellow sharers in all times and places. It is in the eucharist that the community of God's people is fully manifested.

Eucharistic celebrations always have to do with the *whole Church*, and the whole Church is involved in each local eucharistic celebration. In so far as a church claims to be a manifestation of the whole Church, it will take care to order its own life in ways which take seriously the interests and concerns of other churches.

Solidarity in the eucharistic communion of the body of Christ and *responsible care* of Christians for one another and the world find specific expression in the liturgies: in the mutual forgiveness of sins; the sign of peace; intercession for all; the eating and drinking together; the taking of the elements to the sick and those in prison or the celebration of the eucharist with them. All these manifestations of love in the eucharist are directly related to Christ's own testimony as a servant, in whose servanthood Christians themselves participate.

As God in Christ has entered into the human situation, so eucharistic liturgy is close to the concrete and particular situations of men and women. In the early Church the ministry of deacons and deaconesses gave expression in a special way to this aspect of the eucharist. The place of such ministry between the *table* and the *needy* properly testifies to the redeeming presence of Christ in the world.

II. Recommendation: challenge injustice

The eucharist embraces *all aspects of life*. It is a representative act of thanksgiving and offering on behalf of the whole world. The eucharistic celebration demands reconciliation and sharing among all those regarded as brothers and sisters in the one family of God and is a constant challenge in the search for appropriate relationships in social, economic and political life (Matt. 5:23f.; I Cor. 10:16f.; I Cor. 11:20-22; Gal. 3:28). All kinds of injustice, racism, separation and lack of freedom are *radically challenged* when we share in the body and blood of Christ. Through the eucharist the all-renewing grace of God penetrates and restores human personality and dignity. The eucharist involves the believer in the central event of the world's history.

Discussion questions

1. What is the moral dilemma posed in the opening story? Are you able to share the same cup with enemies as well as friends?

2. What does it mean that the Church used the basic essentials of food and drink in a communal meal as its central act of worship? How would you describe the relation between divine justice and human justice, the celebration of the eucharist and the struggles of everyday life?

3. Why is there such a tragic separation between the "spiritual" and the "material" dimensions of life? How does that confuse and weaken Christian responsibility in society?

4. What is the potential economic significance of a trinitarian faith that worships God as Creator of the universe, Christ as our enfleshed (incarnate) Redeemer, and the Holy Spirit as the Sustainer and Renewer of life all around us?

5. Do you remember the story of Ananias and Sapphira (read Acts 5:1-11)? Should we expect Christians in eucharistic communion to be free from motives of self-interest and greed? What does St Paul mean in Romans 7:19-25? What really prompts Christians to respond to the needs of others?

6. Could it be that the energy crisis, endemic hunger, the arms race, along with persistent inflation and unemployment, are all part of an early-warning system, telling the human race that its plundering of the earth's resources cannot continue for ever? How faithfully have Christians interpreted — and obeyed — the biblical command: "... fill the earth and subdue it, and have dominion over every living thing" (Gen. 1:28)?

Ministry

Ministry

Prophets and profits

The TV evening news had shown a protest march against inflation in Bonn, a prison riot in Paris, a water pollution crisis in Frankfurt, more nuclear testing in the Pacific, and a drought in India. The commercials had advertised a tranquillizer, a roomier automobile, a meat product for pets.

One viewer suddenly realized what had been happening to her. The worldwide communications network had laid the world's problems at her feet in colour and action instantly every night for years. She had felt obligated to help solve the problems, but her efforts had seemed so futile. Her conscience had become so overloaded that it had become numb. Maybe that was why she was reacting against any concern.

She reached over, petted her dog, had a slight stab of conscience for having bought the roomier car, but felt good that she wasn't taking tranquillizers.

Yet this viewer was a Christian lawyer and she would have to decide whether to urge her congregation to give to the India project, to join in the church's efforts to secure better laws, or to study the synod statement on nuclear warfare.

She would also have to decide how much to encourage her children to enjoy their personal comforts.

As our awareness of the needs of the world increases, our need for personal escape also increases. How concerned should we be about the world?

How much attention should the church give to (circle):

		Very much	Some	Little	None
a)	Teaching personal salvation and forgiveness	3	2	1	0
b)	Teaching conscience and social responsibility	3	2	1	0
c)	Aiding victims of natural disasters	3	2	1	0
d)	Aiding victims of social injustice	3	2	1	0
e)	Taking political and economic action to fight oppression and plundering of natural resources	3	2	1	0

Ministry (1)

I. The calling of the whole people of God

In a broken world God calls the *whole of humanity* to become God's people. For this purpose God chose *Israel* and then spoke in a unique and decisive way in Jesus Christ, *God's Son*. Jesus made his own the nature, condition and cause of the whole human race, giving himself as a sacrifice for all. Jesus' life of service, his death and resurrection, are the foundation of a *new community* which is built up continually by the good news of the Gospel and the gifts of the sacraments.

The Holy Spirit unites in a single body those who follow Jesus Christ and sends them as witness into the world. Belonging to the Church means *living in communion* with God through Jesus Christ in the Holy Spirit.

The life of the *Church* is based on Christ's victory over the powers of evil and death, accomplished once for all. Christ offers forgiveness, invites to repentance and delivers from destruction. Through Christ, people are enabled to turn in praise to God and in service to their neighbours. In Christ they find the source of new life in freedom, mutual forgiveness and love. Through Christ their hearts and minds are directed to the consummation of the Kingdom where Christ's victory will become manifest and all things made new. God's purpose is that, in Jesus Christ, all people should share in this fellowship.

The Church lives through the liberating and renewing power of the *Holy Spirit*. That the Holy Spirit was upon Jesus is evidenced in his baptism, and after the resurrection that same Spirit was given to those who believed in the Risen Lord in order to recreate them as the body of Christ. The Spirit calls people to faith, sanctifies them through many gifts, gives them strength to witness to the Gospel, and empowers them to serve in hope and love. The Spirit keeps the Church in the truth and guides it despite the frailty of its members.

The Holy Spirit bestows on the community *diverse and complementary gifts*. These are for the common good of the whole people and are manifested in acts of service within the community and to the world. They may be gifts of communicating the Gospel in word and deed, gifts of healing, gifts of praying, gifts of teaching and learning, gifts of serving, gifts of guiding and following, gifts of inspiration and vision. All members are called to discover, with the help of the community, the gifts they have received and to use them for the building up of the Church and for the service of the world to which the Church is sent.

II. Recommendation: ministry of the laity

Christ established a new access to the Father. Living in this communion with God, *all members of the Church are called* to confess their faith and to give account of their hope. They are to identify with the joys and sufferings of all people as they seek to witness in caring love. The members of Christ's body are to struggle with the oppressed towards that freedom and dignity promised with the coming of the Kingdom. This mission needs to be carried out in varying political, social and cultural contexts. In order to fulfill this mission faithfully, they will seek relevant forms of witness and service in each situation. In so doing they bring to the world a foretaste of the joy and glory of God's Kingdom.

Discussion questions

1. How seriously does your church take the diversity of the Spirit's gifts among its lay members? What are some of your own distinctive gifts and abilities? Can you share a recent experience when you felt that you were actively participating in the church's mission and ministry?

2. Can the Gospel be proclaimed best today by words or in deeds? Why? Is the Christian message usually taught or caught? Do you remember any occasions when words and deeds have mutually reinforced each other — at home, on the job, at school, or in recreation?

3. What are the principles of righteousness which the Hebrew prophets spoke of as belonging to the Kingdom of God (discuss Amos 2:6; 5:21-25; Hosea 6:6; 12:6; Isaiah 5:1-24; Micah 6:6-8)?

4. Can we speak of a "Christian" economic system? Which means of production, structures of distribution and patterns of consumption contribute most to human peace, equality and freedom?

5. What is the proper relation between personal charity and social justice in overcoming human suffering? For example, what are considered to be the proper roles of the church, the government, trade unions and other social and economic institutions in shaping public policy in your society?

6. Why is the global gap widening daily between the richer and the poorer nations of the world? The world's resources are intended by God to support human dignity, wholeness, community and liberation. What are the relative benefits and risks of various trade arrangements and aid programmes affecting your region?

7. The churches are biblically committed to the creation of just, participatory and sustainable societies throughout the world. How can this goal be nurtured in the worship and educational life of your congregation? What should be its advocacy efforts on behalf of the oppressed and the exploited in the community?

At home alone

Pastor Gardiner stood thinking for a long while in front of Muriel Johnson's home. He was certainly not looking forward to this particular visit! How, he wondered, can I say what I want to say without sounding defensive?

The last time he called on Mrs Johnson she made it very clear why she stopped coming to church worship: she had found a "deeper religious experience" by watching a popular evangelist on television. From him she received comfort and inspiration. He had also convinced her that going to church wasn't nearly as important as your own personal relation to Jesus.

And that, she decided, was something she could have at home alone without being disturbed in church by all those rowdy children and radical college students and continual demands to help with this charity programme or that fund drive. I can pray very well in my own living room, she told Pastor Gardiner, without needing any minister to lead me, thank you. Besides, some of your sermons aren't very spiritual when they try to "mix religion and politics".

As the pastor walked up to the door, he recalled that Mrs Johnson's daughter and son-in-law had also stopped coming to church. Your services are "too stiff and formal for us", they told him. Why do you repeat those same things week after week, with the same people leading the same worship out of the same book? Frankly, they said, we far prefer our occasional prayer meetings with a small circle of close friends where there is no "expert minister to preach at us".

They're right, the pastor thought, when they say that our church community isn't always as lively as it should be. And it's also true that prayer groups, like Muriel's personal prayers, are an important part of our Christian life.

But yet, he countered, isn't the Church the body of Christ, more than the sum of its isolated scattered parts? Doesn't the Holy Spirit make something special happen when all those people gather together as God's family around the Table of the Lord? Without their common effort, how could we even have begun to support our three refugee families? Chrisitanity isn't a private affair; didn't Christ come to bridge our isolation from each other as well as our separation from God? And isn't it my special vocation, he wondered, to build up and guide our community life with Christ's help? But how could he say all that in a way that would somehow make sense to Muriel Johnson?

In any case, he concluded, it's important that I come here, if only to show that we care enough to listen to her. That, too, is a big part of my role. As he rang the doorbell, Pastor Gardiner took a deep breath. A front window was open and he could already hear the voice of the TV evangelist.

Ministry (2)

I. The ordained ministry

In order to fulfill its mission, the Church needs persons who are publicly and continually responsible for pointing to its fundamental dependence on Jesus Christ, and thereby provide, within a multiplicity of gifts, a *focus of its unity*. The ministry of such persons, who since very early times have been ordained, is *constitutive* for the life and witness of the Church.

The Church has never been without persons holding specific *authority and responsibility*. Jesus chose and sent the disciples to be witnesses of the Kingdom (Matt. 10:1-8). The Twelve were promised that they would "sit on thrones judging the tribes of Israel" (Luke 22:30).

A particular role is attributed to the Twelve within the communities of the first generation. They are witnesses of the Lord's life and resurrection (Acts 1:21-26). They lead the community in prayer, teaching, the breaking of bread, proclamation and service (Acts 2:42-47; 6:2-6, etc.). The very existence of the Twelve and other apostles shows that, from the beginning, there were *differentiated* roles in the community.

The role of the apostles as witnesses to the resurrection of Christ is unique and unrepeatable. There is therefore a *difference* between the apostles and the ordained ministers whose ministries are founded on theirs.

As Christ chose and sent the apostles, Christ continues through the Holy Spirit to choose and call persons into the *ordained ministry*. As heralds and ambassadors, ordained ministers are representatives of Jesus Christ to the community, and proclaim his message of reconciliation. As leaders and teachers they call the community to submit to the authority of Jesus Christ, the Teacher and Prophet, in whom law and prophets were fulfilled. As pastors, under Jesus Christ the Chief Shepherd, they assemble and guide the dispersed people of God, in anticipation of the coming Kingdom.

All members of the believing community, ordained and lay, are *inter-related*. On the one hand, the community needs *ordained ministers*. Their presence reminds the community of the divine initiative, and of the dependence of the Church on Jesus Christ, who is the source of its mission and the foundation of its unity. They serve to build up the community in Christ and to strengthen its witness. In them the Church seeks an example of holiness and loving concern.

On the other hand, the ordained ministry has no existence apart from the *community*. Ordained ministers can fulfill their calling only in and for the community. They cannot dispense with the recognition, the support and the encouragement of the community.

The *chief responsibility* of the ordained ministry is to assemble and build up the body of Christ by proclaiming and teaching the word of God, by celebrating the sacraments, and by guiding the life of the community in its worship, its mission and its caring ministry.

It is especially in the eucharistic celebration that the ordained ministry is the *visible focus* of the deep and all-embracing communion between Christ and the members of his body. In the celebration of the eucharist, Christ gathers, teaches and nourishes the Church. It is Christ who invites to the meal and who presides at it. In most churches this presidency is signified and represented by an ordained minister.

II. The ministry of men and women in the Church

Where Christ is present, human barriers are being broken. The Church is called to convey to the world the image of a new humanity. There is in Christ no male or female (Gal. 3:28). Both women and men must discover together their contributions to the service of Christ in the Church.

The Church must discover the ministry which can be provided by women as well as that which can be provided by men. A deeper understanding of the *comprehensiveness* of ministry which reflects the interdependence of men and women needs to be more widely manifested in the life of the Church.

Though they agree on this need, the churches draw different conclusions as to the admission of *women* to the ordained ministry. An increasing number of churches have decided that there are no biblical or theological reasons against ordaining women, and many of them have subsequently proceeded to do so. Yet many churches hold that the tradition of the Church in this regard must not be changed.

III. Recommendation:
joint study on women's ordination

Some churches ordain both men and women, others ordain only men. Differences on this issue raise obstacles to the mutual recognition of ministries. But those obstacles must *not be regarded as substantive hindrance* for further efforts towards mutual recognition. Openness to each other holds the possibility that the Spirit may well speak to one church through the insights of another. Ecumenical consideration, therefore, should encourage, not restrain, the facing of this question.

The discussion of these practical and theological questions *within* the various churches and Christian traditions should be complemented by *joint study* and reflection within the ecumenical fellowship of all churches.

Discussion questions

1. What is the basic difference between an exclusive emphasis on "saving souls" and involving baptized persons into a local eucharistic community actively engaged in a comprehensive Christian mission of worship, teaching, witness, service and solidarity?

2. How should we properly relate the "royal priesthood" of all baptized believers (I Pet. 2:9) to the ordained ministry of those persons called and set apart in ordination to be the pastors or priests of the Christian community?

3. Why may we say that the ordained ministry helps to constitute the Church and provide a focus for its unity? To whom are priests and pastors accountable? For whom are they responsible? By what authority do they speak and act? With what power, if any, and of what kind, should they exercise their holy calling?

4. What do you consider to be the most important arguments for or against the ordination of women? How can the churches best deal with current issues that were not explicitly treated in the scriptures and tradition of the early Church?

5. In the light of your situation, how would you rank the importance of the many duties of the leader of your Christian community? For enabling the ministry of the laity in and for the world, which of the clergy's activities do you consider to be (a) really essential, (b) beneficial but not really essential, or (c) neither essential nor beneficial?

Through others' eyes

Shemala almost felt defeated as she listened to the public debate. For as long as she could remember, these churches had been negotiating to form a united church in her Asian country, but tonight they sounded as far apart as ever.

First, an Anglican layman had spoken of the importance of bishops. The bishop, he said, is a sign of the Church's unity; bishops provide a link between the local community and the wider Church.

Well, that sounded fine to her, especially since she was Anglican and had grown up with the idea of bishops. But then a Baptist minister spoke of how some bishops acted like kings instead of servants of Christ. Is this really, he asked, the form of ministry we want for our united church? Shouldn't the basic decisions of the Church be made right in the local congregation?

A Methodist minister said he was in favour of bishops even though his church didn't have them now. He pointed out that the ancient Church quickly developed a "threefold" pattern of bishops, local ministers and deacons in order to carry out its ministry. He also reminded the audience that this pattern was already written into their original Plan of Union. Shemala knew this was true. Another Methodist, however, said that they had been arguing over union for so many years that the younger generation knew nothing about the Plan of Union! They would have to be convinced of the need for bishops all over again.

Oh, it was so confusing! She felt that her own priest had made an important point about the need for a continuous tradition of the Church running back to the apostles. The succession of bishops, he said, is a way of guaranteeing this tradition. But that set off an uproar! A Baptist and a Presbyterian both responded that their churches may not have bishops, but they had certainly preserved the truth of the Gospel without them.

I wish, thought Shemala, that these people could see themselves through the eyes of my Buddhist friends. Are Anglican and Methodist churches different religions, her friends had asked her. If not, then why do they seem so divided? These questions hit home, especially since 70% of the people in her country are Buddhist while only 8% are Christian! What kind of witness, she wondered, are we really making?

Finally, Shemala stood up to speak. "Why is it", she asked, "that ministry is always an issue that divides us? Isn't there some way of reconciling our differences? Can't we realize that none of our churches is perfect as it is now?"

Shemala sat down. Well, she thought, at least I've said what I wanted to say. But the debate continued to swirl around her.

Ministry (3)

I. Bishops, presbyters and deacons

The New Testament does not describe a single pattern of ministry which might serve as a blueprint or continuing norm for all future ministry in the Church. In the New Testament there appears rather a *variety of forms* which existed at different places and times.

As the Holy Spirit continued to lead the Church in life, worship and mission, certain elements from this early variety were further developed and became settled into a more universal pattern of ministry. During the second and third centuries, a *threefold pattern* of bishop, presbyter and deacon underwent considerable changes in its practical exercise.

At some points of crisis in the history of the Church, the continuing functions of ministry were in some places and communities distributed according to structures *other than* the predominant threefold pattern. Sometimes appeal was made to the New Testament in justification of these other patterns. In other cases, the restructuring of ministry was held to lie within the competence of the Church as it adapted to changed circumstances.

It is important to be aware of the *changes* the threefold ministry has undergone in the history of the Church. In the earliest instances, where threefold ministry is mentioned, the reference is to the *local* eucharistic community. The bishop was the leader of the community. He was ordained and installed to proclaim the word and preside over the celebration of the eucharist. He was surrounded by a college of presbyters and by deacons who assisted in his tasks. In this context the bishop's ministry was a focus of unity within the whole community.

Soon, however, the functions were modified. Bishops began increasingly to exercise oversight (*episkopé*) over several local communities at the same time. In the first generation, apostles had exercised oversight in the wider

95

Church. Later Timothy and Titus are recorded to have fulfilled a function of oversight in a given area. Later again this apostolic task is carried out in a new way by the bishops. They provide a focus for unity in life and witness within areas comprising *several* eucharistic communities. As a consequence, presbyters and deacons are assigned new roles. The presbyters become the leaders of the local eucharistic community and, as assistants of the bishops, deacons receive responsibilities in the larger area.

Although there is no single New Testament pattern, although the Spirit has many times led the Church to adapt its ministries to contextual needs, and although other forms of the ordained ministry have been blessed with gifts of the Holy Spirit, nevertheless the *threefold ministry* of bishop, presbyter and deacon may serve today as an expression of the *unity we seek* and also as a means for achieving it. Historically, it is true to say, the threefold ministry became the generally accepted pattern in the Church of the early centuries and is still retained today by many churches.

The Church as the body of Christ and the eschatological people of God is constituted by the Holy Spirit through a diversity of gifts or ministries. Among these gifts a ministry of oversight (*episkopé*) is necessary to express and safeguard the unity of the body. Every church needs this *ministry of unity* in some form in order to be the Church of God, the one body of Christ, a sign of the unity of all in the Kingdom.

Today the threefold pattern stands evidently in *need of reform*. In some churches the collegial dimension of leadership in the eucharistic community has suffered diminution. In others, the function of deacons has been reduced to an assistant role in the celebration of the liturgy: they have ceased to fulfill any function with regard to the diaconal witness of the Church.

In general, the relation of the presbyterate to the episcopal ministry has been discussed throughout the centuries, and the degree of the presbyter's participation in the episcopal ministry is still for many an unresolved question of far-reaching ecumenical importance. In some cases, churches which have not formally kept the threefold form have, in fact, maintained certain of its original patterns.

II. Recommendation: threefold ministry of unity

The traditional threefold pattern raises questions for all the churches. Churches *maintaining* the threefold pattern will need to ask how its potential can be fully developed for the most effective witness of the Church in this world. In this task churches *not having* the threefold pattern should also participate. They will further need to ask themselves whether the threefold pattern as developed does not have a powerful claim to be accepted by them.

Discussion questions

1. The opening story illustrates the scandal of divisions within the Church. How valid is it to blame church officials and outdated structures? What about theological professors and traditional doctrine? Do you know of cases where lay people are suspicious of the ecumenical involvement of both church officials and theological professors?

2. The Lima text asks episcopally-structured churches to acknowledge that the New Testament offers no single pattern as a "continuing norm for all future ministry in the Church". It then goes on, nevertheless, to ask non-episcopally structured churches to accept the threefold ministry of bishop, presbyter and deacon as an "expression of the unity we seek and also as a means of achieving it". Is this a defensible ecumenical position?

3. Historical research helps us to discern the many changes that the ministry has undergone throughout the history of the Church. Does this weaken your faith in the providential guidance of the Church by the Holy Spirit?

4. What can be said about the structures and even the titles of bishops, presbyters and deacons in a reformed threefold ministry today? How can bishops best serve as representative pastoral ministers of oversight, continuity and unity in the Church? How can presbyters best serve as pastoral ministers of word and sacraments in a local eucharistic community? How can deacons best represent to the Church its calling as servants in the world?

5. In the history of the Church there have been times when the truth of the Gospel could only be preserved through prophetic and charismatic leaders.

How can the whole community remain attentive to the challenge of such special ministries empowered by the Holy Spirit?

Out of the ashes

The Christian Church exists for a purpose. Its parishes should constantly be renewed to serve that purpose better. If the church described here were yours, what would you want its new programme to be like?

On Friday, Holy Spirit Church had a farewell party for its pastor who left the next day for retirement in Leeds. As the people arrived at worship on Sunday they found that the steeple had been struck by lightning and the church was burning down. The fire not only destroyed the building, but all its membership records, constitutions, council minutes and programme plans, church school materials, and hymnals.

At first people were stunned. Their dear old church and all it stood for seemed gone. As they discussed the situation, however, they gradually realized they had a chance to build a new building as well as an entirely new congregational life.

They would have to decide how to use the insurance money, what parts of the former life of the congregation they would most like to preserve and what parts they would most like to change. Would they build a high tower again?

What programmes would they continue? How would they reconstruct their membership list? When they rewrote their plans, what kind of committees and organization would they have? In all these many tasks, who would lead them, and why?

In your own congregation, what would you try to keep, and what would you change (circle)?

	Kept as is	Changed	Am uncertain
a) Use of building	2	1	0
b) Patterns of worship	2	1	0
c) Forms of ministry	2	1	0
d) Programmes of education	2	1	0
e) Agencies of witness and service	2	1	0
f) Means for determining membership	2	1	0
g) Ways of organizing activities	2	1	0
h) Relations with other churches	2	1	0
i) Other	2	1	0

Ministry (4)

I. Apostolic tradition and episcopal succession

In the Creed, the Church confesses itself to be *apostolic*. The Church lives in continuity with the apostles and their proclamation. The same Lord who sent the apostles continues to be present in the Church. The Spirit keeps the Church in the apostolic tradition until the fulfilment of history in the Kingdom of God.

Apostolic tradition in the Church means *continuity* in the permanent characteristics of the Church of the apostles: witness to the apostolic faith, proclamation and fresh interpretation of the Gospel, celebration of baptism and the eucharist, the transmission of ministerial responsibilities, communion in prayer, love, joy and suffering, service to the sick and the needy, unity among the local churches and sharing the gifts which the Lord has given to each.

The primary manifestation of apostolic succession is to be found in the apostolic tradition of the *Church as a whole*. The succession is an expression of the permanence and, therefore, of the continuity of the Church throughout history; it also underlines the calling of the ordained minister as guardian of the faith.

Where churches see little importance in *orderly transmission*, they should ask themselves whether they have not to change their conception of continuity in the apostolic tradition. On the other hand, where the ordained ministry does not adequately serve the proclamation of the *apostolic faith*, churches must ask themselves whether their ministerial structures are not in need of reform.

Under the particular historical circumstances of the growing Church in the early centuries, the *succession of bishops* became one of the ways, together with the transmission of the Gospel and the life of the community, in which the apostolic tradition of the church was expressed. This succession was understood as serving, symbolizing and guarding the continuity of the apostolic faith and communion.

In churches which practise the succession through the episcopate, it is increasingly recognized that a continuity in apostolic faith, worship and mission has been preserved in churches which have *not retained* the form of historic episcopate. This recognition finds additional support in the fact that the reality and function of the episcopal ministry have been preserved in many of these churches, with or without the title "bishop". Ordination, for example, is always done in them by persons in whom the Church recognizes the authority to transmit the ministerial commission.

These considerations do not diminish the importance of the episcopal ministry. On the contrary, they enable churches which have not retained the episcopate to appreciate the episcopal succession as a *sign*, though not a guarantee, of the *continuity and unity* of the Church.

Today churches, including those engaged in union negotiations, are expressing willingness to *accept* episcopal succession as a sign of the apostolicity of the life of the whole Church. Yet, at the same time, they *cannot accept* any suggestion that the ministry exercised in their own tradition should be invalid until the moment that it enters into an existing line of episcopal succession. Their acceptance of the episcopal succession will best further the unity of the whole Church if it is part of a *wider process* by which the episcopal churches themselves also regain their lost unity.

II. Recommendation:
mutual recognition of ordained ministries

In order to achieve mutual recognition, different steps are required of different churches. For example:

(a) Churches which *have preserved* the episcopal succession are asked to recognize both the apostolic content of the ordained ministry which exists in churches which have not maintained such succession and also the existence in these churches of a ministry of oversight (*episkopé*) in various forms.

(b) Churches *without* the episcopal succession, and living in faithful continuity with the apostolic faith and mission, have a ministry of word and sacrament, as is evident from the belief, practice, and life of those churches. These churches are asked to realize that the continuity with the Church of the apostles finds profound expression in the successive laying on of hands by bishops and that, though they may not lack the continuity of the apostolic tradition, this sign will strengthen and deepen that continuity. They may need to recover the sign of the episcopal succession.

Discussion questions

1. *What does it mean to confess in the creed that the Church is "apostolic"? What is the ecumenical significance of the distinction proposed between (a) the apostolic tradition of the whole Church, and (b) the episcopal succession of the apostolic ministry within the Church?*

2. *Do our doctrinal differences really correspond to our ecclesiastical divisions? Are the differences between the churches still far greater than the differences within them? How much official dogma is essential to the Church's unity and how much theological debate is beneficial to its legitimate diversity?*

3. *Who speaks for the Church? What are the structures for official decision-making and authoritative teaching in your church? How should church leaders go about determining the common mind of the people of God?*

4. *What are the best ways today for ecumenical "convergence statements", such as this Lima text, to be tested, endorsed or improved under the guidance of the Holy Spirit and in fidelity to the scriptures and tradition of the Church?*

5. *How has this study helped you personally to strengthen your own ecumenical understanding and commitment in faithful obedience to Jesus' prayer to the Father, "that they may all be one"?*